California Condors

By Alison Tibbitts and
Alan Roocroft

PUBLISHED BY
Capstone Press
Mankato, Minnesota USA

CIP
LIBRARY OF CONGRESS CATALOGING IN PUBLICATION DATA

Tibbitts, Alison.
    California condors / by Alison Tibbitts and Alan Roocroft.
        p. cm. -- (Animals, animals, animals)
    Summary: Discusses the physical characteristics, behavior, and life cycle of California condors and current efforts to save them from extinction.

    ISBN 1-56065-107-5
    1. California condor--Juvenile literature. [1. California condor.
2. Condors. 3. Rare birds. 4. Wildlife conservation.]
I. Roocroft, Alan. II. Title. III. Series: Tibbitts, Alison.
Animals, animals, animals.
QL696.F33T53   1992
598'.912--dc20   92-9192
                                          CIP

Consultant:
Bill Toone, Curator of Birds
Wild Animal Park
Zoological Society of San Diego

Photo Credits:
California Condor Program, U.S. Fish and Wildlife Service;
Robert Mesta, Coordinator: 3

David Clendenen: Cover, title page, 4, 7, 11, 12, 15, 24, 28, 32, back cover

Noel Snyder: 16, 23

Los Angeles Zoo, Mike Wallace, Curator of Birds: 8, 19, 20, 27

Capstone Press
P.O. Box 669, Mankato, MN, U.S.A. 56002-0669

California condors are free again. A pair is soaring over the mountain tops after a five-year absence. The last wild condor was taken by government permit in 1987. A plan is bringing these birds back from **extinction**.

Condors lived at the time of dinosaurs. They ranged all across North America. They adapted to different foods and climates. Large **prehistoric mammals** disappeared because they could not change. **Mastodons** and **saber-toothed tigers** are gone. Condors are still here.

The birds are part of native American religions. Chumash Indians in California call condors "Xo Xo" (pronounced Ho Ho), meaning "Great Spirit." They believe Xo Xo flies high and near to God. He carries them on his wings to the spirit world when they die.

Spanish explorers were the first Europeans to see condors. Soon, collectors wanted skins, feathers, and eggs. Settlers moving west killed many of the birds. Some used them for target practice.

Condors are **New World vultures**. They do not kill. They live on the flesh of dead animals, called **carrion**. Condors are patient and stand aside for birds of **prey**. They are social and forage in groups. There is no reason to fear them.

Most people have never seen a
condor. These creatures will not
win a beauty contest. They are huge.
Shiny black feathers cover their
bodies. They have rubbery necks
and pink heads with hooked
yellow beaks. They have no sense
of smell. Their long legs end in big,
scaly claws.

Condors are not power flyers. They do not flap their wings. The birds soar and glide like great kites. Their wings lock into a straight and stable line. Wind brushes along their wings. Only the long feathers at each wingtip move. An adult's wing span stretches ten feet. That is as long as a small car.

How do such heavy birds get off the ground? They ride up on warm air currents called **thermals**. Every morning, thermals build along the faces of cliffs where condors roost. About midday, the birds trudge to the edge of the ledge and jump off. Warm currents carry them up several miles. At the top of the thermal, the birds tuck their wings and fall off. They soar and glide at fifty miles an hour.

Condors like remote places far from man. The area's size matters less than its ability to support wildlife. Trees near mountains or grasslands make good roosts. National forests have important nest sites. Condors never depend on one habitat. They go a hundred miles to feed on an open range.

Like all else about them, condors' nesting habits are unusual. They mate for life. Breeding begins with a head-down, wings-out courtship dance. Other condors see them as they soar in search of a good nest site. Their wing tips touch in **pair-flight** while they seek a cave or crevice in a rocky cliff.

The birds are fine parents. One "egg-sits" while the other finds food. They do not build a real nest. The egg lies on the bare dirt floor. It may be **incubated** on a parent's foot. This is risky if the sitter gets up too fast. The pair lays one egg every two years. The time in between is spent raising the chick. Parents teach him what to eat and how to hunt. The chick learns where to live and who his friends are.

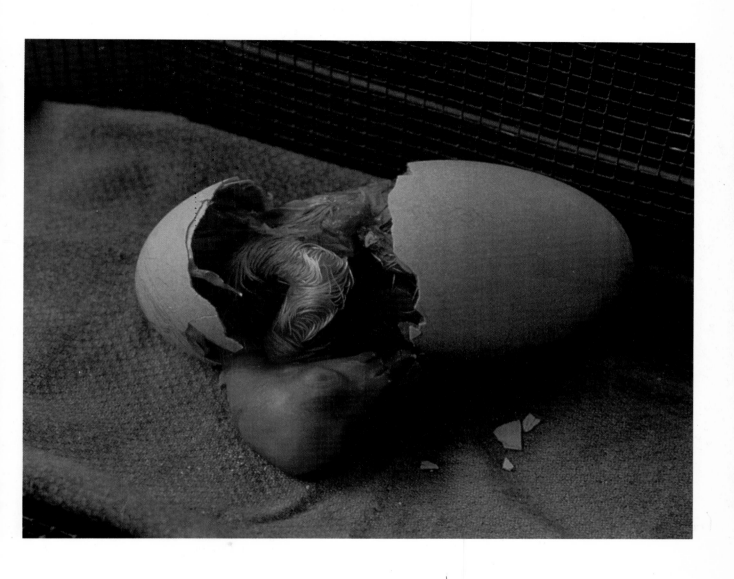

Years ago, field observers noticed the number of condors was going down. **Solar radio transmitters** followed the birds' activity. There was concern the **population** could not survive with so few eggs hatching each year. A plan was started called "**double clutching**." Scientists gently removed the eggs from nests to hatch them in a laboratory. The plan worked. Condors nested again and laid a second egg. Sometimes scientists took that one too. The birds often laid a third egg. Eggs were hatching in both nests and in laboratories.

Scientists worried because some condors were dying from poisoned carrion. The problem had two sources. The first was lead bullets in animals who died after escaping their hunters. The second was **strychnine** used by ranchers to kill animals raiding their herds. Condors picked up these poisons when they fed on **carcasses**. They died slowly and far away from the sources.

The birds needed help. No one could agree what to do before time ran out. On Easter Sunday 1987, a scientist was sad as he "folded the wings of the last wild condor." No one knew if they would be free again.

The Los Angeles Zoo and San Diego Wild Animal Park worked together. They built facilities far from noise and activity. People worked silently and out of the birds' sight. Video cameras and one-way mirrors were used to observe the birds. They bonded with each other and not with people.

Pairs bred regularly in their private enclosures. The population began to increase. Healthy chicks hatched from pale blue eggs the size of avocados. They had fuzzy down and a few bald spots. Dusty gray down grew in at six weeks. Adult feathers sprouted after six months. Molloko was the first chick born from an egg laid in captivity. She came one year after the condors left the wild.

A puppet that looked like an adult condor fed the chicks for six months. It **preened** and played with the babies. Sometimes it "slept" with them. Someday, when there are more condors, chicks will stay with their parents.

The first pair to be released lived together from their third week. They are linked by condor history. The female is Xewe, which means "to cast a shadow." She descends from the last condor to live in the wild. The male is Chocuyens, which means "valley of the moon." His mother was the last female to be captured.

The release was planned carefully. A helicopter flew the birds deep into the mountains. They lived in a special area enclosed by netting. Radio transmitters were attached to record their movements. They had no contact with people studying them. The net came down after two months. Xewe and Chocuyens were free to go.

The giant birds remind us how important it is to **conserve** our world. People must restore damaged **habitats**. This will protect all animals sharing the space.

California condors are not relics coming to the end of their time. They represent nature's silent past. If we allow them to vanish, which species will be next?

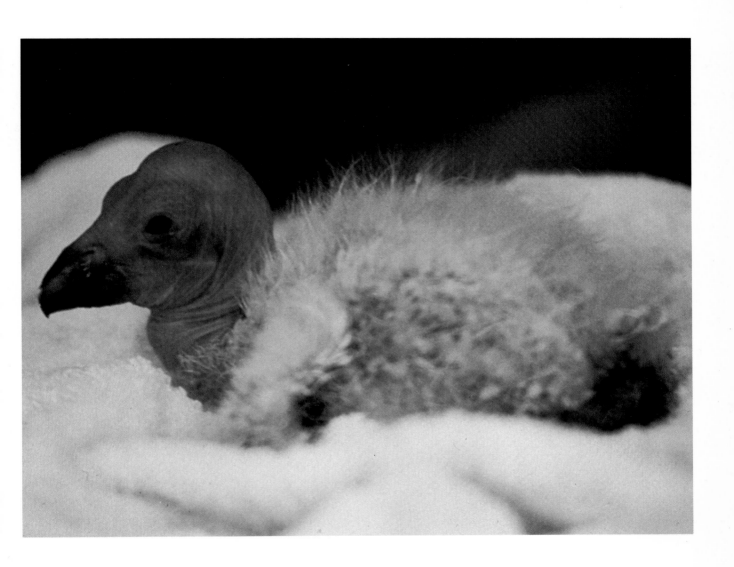

GLOSSARY / INDEX

Carcasses: bodies of dead animals (page 17)

Carrion: dead and decaying flesh (page 6)

Conserve: to guard and protect, to use and manage wisely (page 25)

Double-clutching: an expression which means taking one egg from the nest so the pair of birds will lay another egg (page 17)

Extinction: ceasing to exist, no longer living (page 5)

Habitats: special places to live for a long time (page 25)

Incubate: keep the eggs warm until they hatch (page 14)

Mastodons: giant elephants that lived many thousands of years ago and are now extinct (page 5)

New World vultures: birds of prey living in the western hemisphere countries of North, Central, and South America (page 6)

Pair-flight: two birds flying so close together their wings are almost touching (page 13)

Population: total number of a species, or kind, of animals (page 17)

Preen: a bird's use of its beak to clean and arrange another's feathers (page 21)

Prehistoric mammals: hairy, warm-blooded animals who lived before events were written down as recorded history (page 5)

Prey: an animal hunted and killed by another animal for food (page 6)

Saber-toothed tigers: large cats with long, sharp upper front teeth. They are extinct (page 5)

Solar radio transmitters: radios, powered by the sun, that send and receive messages (page 17)

Strychnine: colorless crystal poison that affects the nervous system and causes death if too much is eaten (page 17)

Thermals: warm air currents that rise due to being heated from below (page 10)